100 WAYS TO *Love* YOUR HUSBAND

LISA JACOBSON

SPIRE

© 2019 by Faithful Families Ministries, LLC

Published by Revell
a division of Baker Publishing Group
PO Box 6287, Grand Rapids, MI 49516-6287
www.revellbooks.com

Spire edition published 2023
ISBN 978-0-8007-4257-7

Previously published in 2014 by Loyal Publishing

Printed in the United States of America

Baker Publishing Group publications use paper produced from sustainable forestry practices and post-consumer waste whenever possible.

23 24 25 26 27 28 29   7 6 5 4 3 2 1

This book is dedicated to our four lovely daughters who bring me such joy and friendship. My hope is that they will someday have the same kind of lasting, loving marriage that their dad and I are so blessed to enjoy.

100 Ways to Love Your Husband

So how did you know he was *the one*? The one you wanted to spend the rest of your life with? That's what the girls were asking me. How did you know Dad was *the guy*?

I felt I should have had an answer ready on the tip of my tongue. A thoughtful insight of some kind. But mostly I just remember him walking into the dinner party with his confident stride, wearing a thick, manly sweater, black Levi's, and Western boots. He was tall, dark, and handsome, with deep blue eyes.

But that doesn't really explain anything.

I mean, no one simply falls in love with a pair of boots . . . do they?

No, it was more than that. Way more than that. It was the way our eyes connected and how we got lost in conversation the moment we sat down together. The way we talked about traveling in France, my experiences in West Africa, and how we both loved Chopin and the same Billy Joel song. We could have talked forever . . . except that our hostess called us to dinner, abruptly reminding us that there were other people in the world. Or at least other people in the room. So I had to settle for staring at him from across the table.

Because by then I knew.

I was looking at the man I was going to marry. He was the one I wanted to spend the rest of my life with—talking, laughing, and loving together. My happily ever after. My very own Mr. Right.

But I had yet to learn that meeting the right guy is one thing—and loving him year after year is quite another. That marrying him would turn out to be both an amazing adventure and a significant challenge. A relationship like no other. I would discover that finding Mr. Right is not a one-way ticket to happiness but only the beginning of a lifelong journey of learning to love each other.

Maybe you're on your own journey—you're newly married, have been together for decades, or still waiting to meet the one God has for you. If so, then I'd like to share a few wonderful ways to love that man of yours.

All right, more than a few. More like one hundred ways.

Always choose love.

Above all things. And not the sentimental, feel-good kind of love, but the kind of love that puts the other person first. The kind that bears all things, believes all things, hopes all things, and endures all things. This is the powerful, persuasive love that leads to a rich and lasting marriage. (Take the time to open your Bible and slowly read 1 Corinthians 13. Here you'll find the most profound description of love ever written.)

Greet him with a *loving* smile.

Who wouldn't enjoy coming home to a loving smile every night? Even if you are tired too or have something else on your mind, put that aside for just a while to make his day wonderful with your warm, loving smile. There are not many smiles in the world these days, so let yours be one of the few and the best in his life.

Let the little things *go*.

Don't hang on to small annoyances. So many marriages slowly deteriorate over the smallest, silliest things. He doesn't take out the trash? He snores at night? He's terrible about leaving the laundry on the floor? It's not all that big of a deal. Just put it behind you and get on with loving him instead.

Work through the **BIG** things.

Take the time to talk through the big problems. Yes, it might mean some hard work and long hours, but it will be worth it. Don't let the things that really matter go. It's worth the effort to address them and deal with them. Otherwise, you're left with a shallow and/or hurting relationship. No way. Go deep.

Don't try *to* CHANGE him.

He's a good man just as he is. He might have room to grow—but then again, so do you. Leave that work to the Holy Spirit. He (the Spirit) is always so much more effective than we'll ever be. So don't make it your job to transform him; simply love him.

6

PRAY
for him.

Make it your daily ministry to lift him up before your heavenly Father. He needs a praying wife. Ask God to protect him and to protect your marriage. Ask for blessing and for mercy. What better gift can a wife offer her husband than her faithful prayers for him?

Remember, he's *not* your girlfriend.

He won't always understand or relate, so don't have unreasonable expectations. Often we want him to "get" what it is we are feeling or struggling with. But he isn't "me" and never will be (thank goodness!). He is made differently with a different experience and different strengths and weaknesses. Don't demand that he be something he can never be.

But be SURE
he's your *best* friend.

Invest in your friendship. Find activities you both enjoy and spend time together. Do the kinds of things friends do: talk, laugh, work, and play. Share your heart with him. Talk about your hopes and dreams, and ask about his too.

Decide in the beginning that you're going to *stick together* until the very end.

You're both in this relationship for the long haul. 'Til death do you part.

And the two shall become one flesh; so then they are no longer two, but one flesh. Therefore what God has joined together, let not man separate. (Mark 10:8–9 NKJV)

Be a
wise woman.

Your husband relies on your wisdom. He needs to know he can count on you for good advice and keen insight. You can—and should—be a wonderful resource for him.

She openeth her mouth with wisdom. (Prov. 31:26)

Look for
l i t t l e   w a y s
to *delight* him.

Be mindful of those small preferences of his. My husband likes his coffee cup warmed up before coffee is poured into it. He has a certain way he likes his T-shirts folded (yes, I'm serious). He likes it when we go to bed at the same time. They might be tiny details, but they say something big to him. What about your guy? What are the things that say love to him?

Allow him
to MAKE
mistakes.

Don't hold them against him. The adage "Everyone makes mistakes" applies to husbands too. If he forgets something? Messes up? Doesn't follow through? It's frustrating, I know, but couldn't we all use some grace? And some of us more than others.

Keep the passion *burning*.

Start a small kitchen fire.

I could hear his footsteps.

Unmistakable. Firm, solid feet. Man-steps. Quite different from the quick pattering of all the little feet I'd heard throughout the day.

Madly chopping and slicing, I never even looked up when he entered.

I felt frantic and stressed, knowing everyone was very hungry and I was very far behind in my dinner preparations. My intentions had been good, it's only that I hadn't anticipated that broken glass earlier in the afternoon. Nor the quarrel between the two children that soon followed. All this took time. Then that last urgent phone call put me hopelessly behind schedule.

And that's how he found me. Madly chopping and slicing.

He came up behind me, slipping his strong arms around my waist, and leaned into me. I should have felt electricity, but mostly I felt annoyance. Irritation. He was slowing me down.

I could immediately sense his disappointment. Could feel his arms drop. Without missing so much as a chop, I tried to explain as I kept prepping away. Explain about the day and all its stresses and frustrations. How behind I was in . . . well, in just about everything. I thought it might help him understand.

He understood, all right. He understood that those carrots took precedence over him. That I was so busy and my tasks so important that I didn't have a minute to acknowledge him. I couldn't even be bothered to turn around.

But I wanted him to know that it was simply a matter of timing. I just wasn't ready for love at that moment.

Wasn't ready for love?

Did that really come from my mouth? From *my heart*?

The man needed his dinner, no doubt. But what did he need even more? A warm, welcoming wife. I was so worried about filling his stomach that it seemed I forgot about filling his heart.

But what if . . . what if I'd done it different? What if I had dropped those carrots, swept the celery aside, turned around, clasped my hands around his neck, and . . . well . . .

Leaned into him?

Stopped my whole world and interrupted my hectic schedule and important plans. To love on him.

What then?

Then he and I could have started a small kitchen fire.

So what does a husband really need? More than dinner, he needs your eyes to light up when he enters the room. He needs to know how thrilled you are that he's come home. How your heart leaps because you two are together again.

He needs a warm, welcoming wife.

So very warm that the two of you alone could start a small kitchen fire.

Confide
in him.

Share with him your thoughts, your dreams, your struggles, and your aspirations. Never keep anything from him. Maybe other people go through life feeling isolated and alone, but don't let yourself be one of those people. Seek his counsel and his comfort. Let him know how much you need and appreciate his friendship.

Don't be surprised **when faced** with a **TRIAL.**

It's not something to tiptoe around, but something to walk through. So walk through it together. At some point, either he or you—or both of you—will encounter a serious bump in the road. Maybe even a serious bump in your relationship. The shock can lead you to give up or want to turn around. But don't let it. Trials come in life and marriage, so prepare yourself for the inevitable.

Enjoy the
MAN he is.

Don't compare him to anyone else. There is little more destructive than hoping he'll become like someone he isn't—whether you say it aloud or think it silently in your head. Instead, make the most of his own unique qualities.

Be quick
to *admit*
when you're wrong.

Don't waste a minute holding on to your pride. Okay, so I've been terrible at this one. I just hate to be wrong! But what a silly way to live—and to love. So what if you're wrong? Just say so and get it over with. It's not as bad as it might first sound.

NEVER leave off
with the *romance*.

It might not be the foundation of your love, but romance sure makes for good glue. Don't let your marriage get stuck in the same old boring routine. Spice it up with some fun and romance!

And romance doesn't have to look like it does in the movies (I actually like our way even better). Maybe you do simple, sweet things—like take a walk in the park or sip tea on the porch. Make time for a regular date night that involves just the two of you talking and enjoying each other.

Be *sweet* to him.

He'll always be glad for a little sweetness. There's such strength found in it. And it's something not commonly found in our harsh world today. Be that refreshing, soul-stirring voice in his ear (see Song of Sol. 2:14).

Care about your appearance.

Not out of vanity but in an effort to put forth your best. Why not freshen up before you see him? Slip on that lovely blouse he often compliments you on. Brush out your hair and pretty up a bit. Such a simple way to communicate to him that you care how you look.

PROTECT
your marriage.

Set up safeguards together to keep things and people from harming what you've got. If you have something you treasure, you watch over it and are willing to defend it.

This doesn't necessarily mean you are insecure, paranoid, or controlling. This simply means you care deeply about your marriage and recognize that we live in a wicked world and you have an enemy who seeks to tear your marriage apart.

Please don't misunderstand.

I trust my husband. Implicitly.

Quite honestly, he's never given me any reason to doubt him. So you can see why it caught him off guard when I voiced my concern.

I told him I was uneasy about the lunch plans he had for that day. He was meeting one of his clients at The Gallery, where they serve up some of the best fajitas in our small town. It was the usual kind of appointment, nothing special. As a literary agent, he often meets with authors to go over their books and contracts. It's all part of the job.

Except this particular client happened to be a woman—an intelligent and attractive woman—and it felt a bit funny to me.

I'm not saying I was downright jealous . . . merely *uncomfortable* with the plan.

Then he reminded me that the lunch was taking place in a public restaurant. That he was in no way drawn to this woman. That he would always and forever be faithful to me.

And I believed him.

But it didn't change how I felt about the meeting.

Now maybe you're wondering if I've watched too many movies (perhaps). Or you suspect I have certain trust issues (not that I know of). Or maybe—just *maybe*—I've observed a number of marital tragedies around us over the years and have grown slightly paranoid. That's a distinct possibility.

Well, in any case, I sure didn't like it. Here's how I put it to him:

Okay, let's go with the fact that you and I are happily married. But what about her? What if she isn't so happily married? What if she finds *you* rather attractive? Strong and sensitive? Hmm . . . (trying not to get too emotional). That would be a bad thing too, wouldn't it?

Then what if nothing "happens"? How about what other people might say who noticed the two of you dining together? Those who watched her throw back her head and laugh at your witty jokes? What rumors would start then?

Yes, what then?

So we talked about it for a long time. A very long time. And in the end we came up with a policy that we both agreed on, and we established not so much rules, as principles, on how we would protect our marriage.

Because our love is worth watching over.

Kiss him
on the lips.

Every day. For a long time. This should be a lifelong practice. My husband's parents have been married for over sixty years and they still kiss on the lips. Makes me smile every time.

Speak well of him to others.

Never put him down or make a slight. Emphasize his strong points and all the many things you appreciate about him. Never let anyone doubt you're his biggest fan. He'll be grateful to you for this.

Be *willing* to
LISTEN.

For many of us, this means we need to be willing to stop talking. To be quiet and to be patient, waiting for him to get his thoughts together. Or maybe it's simply a matter of proving to him that we really want to hear what he has to say. Be quick to hear (see James 1:19).

Make *loving* him your priority.

Above your work. Above your "lists." And even above your children. After your relationship with Christ, your relationship with your husband is the most important relationship in your life and it should be reflected in the decisions you make with both your time and your energy.

DON'T
go to bed angry.

So maybe there's not been the time or opportunity to resolve the issue, but determine to set it aside to work it through at a later time. Make sure you say good night, knowing that—even still—you love each other.

Let not the sun go down upon your wrath. (Eph. 4:26)

Be honest.

It's important to speak the truth—in love—to him. Always. Don't compromise with half-truths or little secrets. Speak straight and true, even when it is difficult to do.

Be
STRONG
for him.

He needs to know he can count on you. Let Christ be your strength, and surprise him with how you can pull through for him.

Strength and honour are her clothing. (Prov. 31:25)

Let him know
when you're
feeling weak.

Sometimes he might need to be reminded that you are a woman, after all. It's not intended as an excuse or a crutch, but be willing to be vulnerable when you need his help or extra support (see 1 Pet. 3:7).

Be trustworthy.

Be that safe place he can turn to, knowing he can count on your understanding and discretion. Prove to him that *your* heart is the perfect place to entrust *his* heart.

The heart of her husband safely trusts in her. (Prov. 31:11 NKJV)

High Tides Grill.

That was the name of the restaurant. I can even remember what I ordered that night: Scallops Provençal, cooked in butter, garlic, lemon, white wine . . . but I'd better stop there. Fresh seafood is considered something of a specialty here in the Pacific Northwest and High Tides Grill is known for some of the best.

So my husband and I were very willing to meet our long-time friends there for dinner. We all enjoyed a lovely evening together—good food and good fun. Both friends have a terrific sense of humor and my sides ached by the end of our time with them.

Still laughing as we climbed into the car to go home, I noticed my husband was unusually quiet. So I asked him, "Tired, honey?"

No, that wasn't it.

Then it occurred to me. "Are you upset?"

He didn't answer, but my instincts told me yes. "Oh," I added sympathetically. "Did John say something that bothered you?" (Although he was rather funny, he could be offensive at times too.)

No, that wasn't it either.

Hmm. I thought about it for a minute or so. "It's not *me*, is it? Did I do something?"

My mind raced through the entire evening, trying to think of what I could have said or done to have offended him. I drew a blank.

But after I asked a few questions, we began discussing it. In all our joking around that night, we got to teasing my husband about one of his quirky characteristics. It was all in fun and friendship, mind you.

Or so I thought.

But my husband—the man I love—didn't appreciate this kind of humor. Not one bit. In particular, he didn't appreciate *my participation* in it.

Please understand, it was never my intention to hurt him. Or dishonor him.

But that was what I'd done. Both of those. And I felt simply terrible for having done so. It was wrong and the opposite of what I truly thought about him.

Something of *a low-tide moment* in our marriage.

I asked his forgiveness, of course, and he gave it. But I decided then and there that I never wanted to do anything like that again.

My husband needs to know that he can count on me to always speak well of him in front of others. That he didn't have to be concerned about "what I'd say next" to other people. That I'd never again look for that little laugh—at his expense.

That he could trust me.

Because I have my husband's heart. It's in my hands and not to be treated lightly or carelessly. Like I did that night. No. He needs to know his heart is safe with me.

Sometimes, as wives, we can forget that his heart is in our hands for safekeeping. We have this incredible privilege to look after him—in public, as well as in private—and that's something to take quite seriously.

His heart is safely tucked in mine.

Make **HIS**
priorities
your own.

Bump them up to the top of your list. What's important to him should be important to you. It's part of putting others' interests before your own (see Rom. 15:1 3).

Lovingly
bear with him.

He'll have his faults. As will you. Recently, one of our daughters asked us why he and I rarely "fight" with each other. My husband's answer? "She doesn't let the irritating things I do bug her."

Well, at least not too much. *Wink.* (See Ephesians 4:2.)

Give *grace.*

He'll need you to extend him grace from time to time. Maybe he doesn't deserve it, but isn't that what grace is all about? When you stop to think about how much grace God has shown you in your times of need, it will help inspire you to shower your husband with the same kind of compassion (see Eph. 2:8–9).

Seek to be
servant-hearted.

Take pleasure in serving him. Yes, really. This might not be the "in thing" right now—you know, to put yourself in a servant's role. But it's a very Christian concept and a real winning one.

By love serve one another. (Gal. 5:13)

Be filled
with *joy*.

It is His joy that remains in us that makes our joy full.

~A.B. Simpson

There's nothing quite so contagious as joy. It sets the tone of your home and of your relationship. Find your joy in God and then let it overflow into all that you do.

Put your
HOPE
in the *Lord.*

When you put your hope in your circumstances, the future, or even in your relationships, you'll always be disappointed. There's only one place to put all your hope—in your God and Creator (see Ps. 71:5).

Give yourself
r o o m
to *grow*.

Love is not perfect—it's just loving. We can be too quick to give up on ourselves when we don't get it right. Or when we fail . . . yet again. But love is a growing thing; it's less an achievement than it is a journey.

Fall asleep
in his arms.

Whenever possible.

Show him
respect.

I've even heard it said that a man would rather feel unloved than disrespected.

A little hard to believe, isn't it? But apparently it's true—respect is very high on a man's list. So you have a twofold challenge: one, decide you will respect him, and two, figure out the kinds of things that communicate respect to him.

Respect has a language all its own. Now it's a matter of becoming fluent in it.

Let him *care* for you.

It's his job. For some reason, the current culture rejects this notion that a man has the responsibility of caring for his wife and reasons instead that she is perfectly capable of taking care of herself. Which is probably true. But why stop or prevent him from caring for you? A man caring for his woman is a beautiful thing.

Set aside
date nights.

Whether you stay home or go out, make sure to consistently put a date night on the calendar. Be willing to get creative if you have scheduling challenges.

We've done everything from having a regular "Friday morning breakfast" date to a "Sunday night errand" date. Even a "put the children to bed early and then head to the back bedroom" date. Whatever you do, set aside specific time to be together.

Admire him.

If you believe he's a real "winner," then he will be one. A man can go far and achieve great things when he has a good woman behind him, cheering him on.

How can a man learn to love when he feels like a loser?

That's what I heard my husband mutter to himself after we left the home of these dear friends who'd been struggling in their marriage.

But his sympathy somewhat surprised me. I suppose I'd taken the wife's "side" since the husband had committed a number of irritating and inconsiderate offenses. He was the one to blame as far as I was concerned.

So that seemed a strange question for my husband to ask and it made me pause.

A *loser*? The man we were talking about had a good job. A nice car. Three precious children. An attractive, talented wife.

No, this guy was no loser.

"Ahem . . . honey? Help me understand here," I said.

He explained and it certainly gave me something to think about.

A man feels "successful" when he knows his woman is behind him—no matter what his accomplishments may be. He needs to know that she believes in him. That she thinks he's a terrific husband (not perfect—just terrific). A first-rate guy. And, if they have children, that he's a fine dad too. That she thinks the world of him, even though he might mess up or make mistakes.

Then I stared at my own husband. I looked at him for a good, long time. Wondering.

Does my man feel successful?

I married a winner and I know it. To me it's quite obvious and I've always figured he knew it too. He has many wonderful qualities that I love and appreciate. But, surely, he was aware of all that.

"Aren't you, honey?"

A slight hesitation. One that shouldn't have been there. One that made my heart drop for a minute. It seemed that I hadn't quite convinced him yet. Well, that needed to change.

It doesn't really take all that much to shower him with your confidence in his success. Just celebrate his strengths and he'll be all the better for it.

I'm sure hoping there'll be no more hesitation around here. Not if I can help it.

Because, babe, you're the champion of my heart. A true winner. And I thank God for you.

Keep having *fun* together.

For the rest of your lives. A little bit of fun can go a long way in building a good marriage.

Keep in mind that *marriage* can be HARD WORK.

But it's so worth it. A good marriage doesn't just happen by itself. It requires that you invest heavily in your relationship. You will need to put time and effort into understanding each other and learning how to walk together.

Do him *good*.

For the rest of your lives together.

> She will do him good and not evil all the days of her life.
> (Prov. 31:12)

Speak only those things that *edify*.

Commit to carefully saying those things that will edify or encourage him. In other words, just because you have a thought or a feeling doesn't mean you should speak it aloud. Rather, take a moment to consider whether what you have to say is going to help the other person or improve the situation. (See Ephesians 4:29.)

Sometimes *the best thing* is to not say a n y t h i n g at all.

Words are not always necessary and can even get in the way of what you're hoping to accomplish. A wise woman knows when she should wait to speak or never even mention it at all.

Stand by him.

Your loyalty is invaluable to him. If he has people in his life who doubt or flat-out disbelieve in him, let them know—loudly and clearly—that you're sticking by his side.

Show appreciation for the many things he does.

For both the big and the small things. Don't take for granted all that he does for you and your home. And if it seems like he's not doing enough? One of the best ways to encourage him to do even more is to be grateful for the stuff he is already doing.

Be a *kind* wife.

Kind words can have a powerful impact on your marriage. Speak gentle, thoughtful things to this man you love, even in those times when he doesn't necessarily deserve it. Maybe even *especially* in those times. It's possible to completely turn around a situation by returning harsh or unjust words with a sweet response. Try it and you might be surprised by the power of kindness.

And on her tongue is the law of kindness. (Prov. 31:26 NKJV)

It all began in a café. Like so many of the meaningful moments in my life.

He and I were sitting together over a grande latte in the newly opened Starbucks at the Green Hills Mall when my dear friend Susan walked in.

My face lit up as soon as I spotted her. She and I had only known each other for a short time, but we'd made an immediate connection the minute we met. Soul sisters. Our young family had recently moved to Nashville and I'd felt rather alone up until then. Being with her was like a breath of fresh air.

So I shot her my sunniest smile. "Hey, girlfriend! C'mon over!"

We exchanged a big hug before both of us began bubbling over with all the latest news. I complimented her on her new dress, told her how much I liked the way she was wearing her hair, thanked her for the book she'd lent me, and emphasized how glad I was to see her.

At some point, I noticed how subdued my husband had become. I waited until she'd left us, then I asked him what was up. Something was clearly on his mind. I could tell that much.

He said it so softly, I barely heard him. "I wish you'd do that for me."

"Okay," I said. "I don't mean to be difficult, but do what?"

"Light up with a sweet smile. Speak kindly and say nice things."

No further explanation was needed. I knew *exactly* what he was talking about. And he was right. I was all smiles for Susan. But in all honesty? I didn't offer too much of this kind of thing to my husband. In fact, I saved my grumpies for him. I rarely bothered with the niceties anymore and was not particularly gracious or polite. He was supposed to love me "just the way I was." No frills or syrup for him.

But it was hurtful for him to see me put on my "sweet face" for everyone else—everyone except the man to whom I'd pledged my lifelong love. Here I was handing out the big smiles and warm compliments to my new friend but dribbling out the tired frowns and whiny complaints to him.

Something's not quite right about that.

Now don't feel badly if you're cringing. I cringed too. Felt somewhat sickened, really. Definitely convicted.

So, girlfriend, that's what got me thinking.

If we're putting on our brightest smiles for our sisters? If we're saving our warmest words for our friends? If we're sharing our kindest thoughts with the girls? Then we might want to consider how hard it must be for him to watch.

Maybe he doesn't mention it, but my guess is that he'd appreciate it if we showed some of that warmth and kindness to him too.

So even if he's around most every day, why not light up when he walks in the room? Tell him how handsome he's looking today. How glad you are to see him. Give him a big hug and maybe a bit more.

Put on your sweet face and say nice things.

Be like a breath of fresh air to him.

Be a kind wife.

Make
his *dreams*
your *dreams.*

Treasure them like your own. Ask him about what he hopes to do someday and let him know you believe in his dreams—and him. Plan out together the steps you can take to make those dreams come true.

LOOK
into
each other's
eyes.

Adoringly, each and every day.

Be *extravagant* in your love.

Go big. Pour out your heart generously and enthusiastically. If you want an amazing marriage, then start by showering him with amazing love.

Allow for hormonal fluctuations.

But don't make it an excuse for sin. Feeling edgy? Snappish? Droopy? It tends to come with the territory—just avoid taking it out on him. It's not really his fault, after all.

Speak his
love language—
what says love
to him.

And speak it often! Ask him the kinds of things that make him feel loved by you. He might have an answer ready or he might not. If not, then ask if he'll think about it.

Also, you can study him and watch for those things that seem to fill him up. Then make sure you do those things for him or say the words that make him feel loved.

Don't make
accusations.

Ask questions, but don't begin with blame, which will immediately put him on the defensive. Instead, begin a conversation that gives him a chance to explain his perspective or actions.

Aren't there two sides to every story? What we thought was the case might not be as it appears. Give him the benefit of the doubt.

Fear the *Lord*.

And you'll be honored.

But a woman who fears the Lord, she shall be praised.
(Prov. 31:30 NKJV)

Intertwine your lives wherever possible.

Run errands, go for walks, curl up on the couch. Just seek to be together. Don't wait for date night to find things you share in common.

A good friend recently confessed something to me.

She struggled with jealousy.

Of me.

Really . . . jealous of me? How could that be? We've been friends for many years and she knows I've had my share of grief and trials. Nothing was overly amazing about my life.

What was there to be jealous of?

Then she came out with it: she was envious of the kind of husband I had. She wished hers was more like mine. I could only stare at her. I sure didn't get it.

So she clarified. She couldn't help but notice how much time my husband and I spent with each other. The two of us were often found together—working in the yard, going for a walk, sitting at the café, or maybe standing in line at Costco.

But we were always together. Life wasn't like that with her husband. The two of them lived functional but basically separate lives. And she wished they had what we had. If only they were as closely connected as we were. *If only her husband was like mine.*

Now it was my turn to confide.

All that time we spend together? It's not only because of him. It's also because of me.

Yes, it's true. I'm nearly shameless when it comes to orchestrating time together. Any excuse will do. I'll do whatever I can to get close to him.

This used to bother me. Bug me. Discourage me. But it doesn't anymore. I came to realize that I'd rather be with him—even if that was my doing—than apart from him.

So it can be up to me to make the move.

If I smell coffee brewing in the morning (that man wakes up waaaay too early, if you ask me), I'll drag myself out of my comfy covers to have a cup with him before he dives into his work.

Close to him.

If he's off to run errands, I'll run out to the truck and ask if I can come along. He'll give me a grin and tell me to hop on in. Who cares if he's only going to the farm supply store? It's a chicken-feed date and I'll take it.

Close to him.

If he's working in the garden, I'll throw on a pair of old jeans and join him out in the green bean patch. We both weed. I talk the entire time. And he listens (*I think*).

Close to him.

And if it's the end of the night and he announces he's heading to bed? Well, I'll give him a wink and tell him to wait up 'cause I'm coming too.

Really close to him.

Start each day
with a
smile and a *kiss.*

What better way to begin? Set the tone for the day with a simple gesture of love for each other.

Go to the
WORD
when things seem dark.

The Bible will be a lamp to your feet and a light to your path (see Ps. 119:105). Even when all seems black and rather bleak, there is always hope to be found in the Word of God. When you don't know what to do next or where to turn? Turn to His Word.

Give him *all* your heart.

Not only a part of it. It's so tempting to hold out and to pull back, but don't play it safe. Be willing to go all the way with him. Sure, it's a risk. But the two of you are one now and your heart . . . is his heart.

Forgive.

A happy marriage is the union of two good forgivers.

~Ruth Bell Graham

This is one of the truest statements ever made. Decide you're not only going to be his lover—you're going to be his forgiver. Be quick to forgive and get good at it. You'll probably have lots of opportunities to practice it.

Then forget.

Once an offense has been forgiven, put it behind you and never pick it back up again. Here's the hard part: letting go. Resist the temptation to grab that ugly or hurtful thing back and maybe even throw it at him when he repeats the behavior. I'm sorry, but this doesn't count as true forgiveness. Forgive as God has forgiven you —as far as the east is from the west (see Ps. 103:12).

Cling to each other
in the
hard times.

Don't let trials pull you apart. Instead, be sure they bring you closer together. This decision is best made before the trial comes.

When our daughter was born with severe brain damage, the hospital warned us that most marriages don't make it through a tragic situation like ours. That thought terrified me. So we looked at each other and decided—right then and there—we were going to stick together through it.

Share interests.

As many as possible. See how you can join him in his hobbies and invite him to share in yours.

Even if you don't both enjoy the same things, at the very least you can be enthusiastic about what interests him. And then look for activities you can learn to enjoy together as well. Start something new if you have to.

Don't let
FEAR
hold you back.

Take risks and step out together. Fear can have a powerful grip on your life and your marriage. But this is the voice of the enemy—it's never from the God who made you and set you free.

For God had not given us a spirit of fear, but of power and of love and of a sound mind. (2 Tim. 1:7 NKJV)

Laugh at his jokes.

Yes, even if you've heard those jokes before. Laugh because he's funny (or trying to be) and laugh because laughter is healing.

Remember
the one you
fell in *love* with.

Don't let him get lost in the dailiness of life.

And if you've become distracted and weighed down, take some time off to renew your love for each other. Take a holiday. Slow down. Or simply remind yourself that he is the one you love.

Fix his *favorite* foods.

You know what they say about the way to a man's heart . . .

Listen
sympathetically
as he tells you
about his day.

Sometimes being a friend means caring about the little things—and the big things—that go on in his world. Put aside time and make it a priority to hear about what goes on with him. Spending those simple moments together creates little connecting points that add up over time.

Put your
love for God
FIRST.

The most loving thing you can do for your husband is to invest in your relationship with your God above all.

Reach out
and *touch*.

A tender touch can do so much good—for you both. Even when things aren't going too well, sometimes this one simple but loving gesture can soften spirits and ease the tension.

Remember that you are a POWERFUL *influence* in his life.

"Fifty Women of Influence."

That's what was featured on the cover of the magazine. The fifty faces of women who've been recognized as having significant influence. A truly impressive collection.

So I don't know why that magazine cover had this effect on me, but I looked at those fifty women and immediately felt small. Inconsequential. Unknown.

A nobody.

Because, of course, my picture will never be on the front of that magazine. Not that I've ever aspired to such a place. But still . . .

I was somehow struck by my insignificance.

I know it's not right—or even reasonable—for me to think this way. Yet that cover managed to stir up so many of my insecurities and self-doubts that I began questioning whether I'd do *anything* meaningful with my life. Ever.

After all, who am I? No one, really.

The dark, defeating doubts swirled around as I brewed a fresh pot of coffee for my husband and continued with me as I trudged up the stairs to his home office. I poured him a cup and then began pouring out my "pitiful me" thoughts before him. Poor, meaningless me. I was jabbering on and on about how I had never amounted to much and probably never would, when suddenly and unexpectedly my pity party came to a complete stop.

I realized that my husband wasn't paying the least bit of attention to me. He wasn't listening at all, but he was smiling at something in front of him. What? What was distracting him?

Then I saw it. Right smack in the middle of his desk sat a nicely framed photograph of his beloved wife.

Yes, that would be *me*.

Nobody else. Not one single photo of the fifty women of influence was placed before him. Just little, simple, wifey me.

And then came the moment of revelation: *I am a woman of influence.* Tremendous influence. You see, it's my face that's featured on the cover of his life.

Because amazingly enough, the Lord has chosen *this* woman to be *that* man's wife. Which means it's me—and only me—who completes him.

- Who recognizes his strengths.
- Who balances out his weaknesses.
- Who builds him up.
- Who understands him like no one else.

- Who encourages him when he's down or discouraged.
- Who sleeps by his side at night.
- Who stands behind him.
- Who brings out the best in him.
- Who loves him for who he is.

It had never occurred to me before, but I'm a woman of great influence.

But you know what else? So are you.

You also are a woman of consequence and have a powerful role to play in your husband's life. You are the most influential woman in his world. And to my way of thinking, that is one of the highest honors and privileges a woman can hold.

So it looks like I *am* significant—even if it's only in the eyes of one man. Yet he's the one man who matters most in my life. My photograph is placed prominently where all the world can see it. Or better yet—where he can see it.

A powerful woman of influence.

Know that
marriage
is like a long,
s l o w   w a l k
together.

More a marathon than a sprint. So just keep walking. Together.

Communicate *confidence* in who he is and what he's about.

This communication is so powerful in your man's life. He needs to hear your cheers more than you might realize. And he probably needs to hear them louder and more often than might be evident. So speak words of belief and assurance that he has much to offer the world.

Throw a little *surprise* in there.

Every once in a while. Just for fun. Spice it up with something unexpected. I love the look on my husband's face when I do something out of the ordinary that he didn't see coming.
   Surprise!

TIMING
can make all
the difference
in the world.

Discuss difficult things when you're both rested—and fed.
Often these simple things can determine whether the dis-
cussion will become a heated argument or a profitable conversation.

Work *together.*

In the garage, the kitchen, the garden, or the barn, it's always more fun with two. Find ways you can join efforts to get things done. Help him out with his work, his chores, or his honey-do list. And then let him do the same for you.

Let him know
w h a t   y o u   n e e d
from him.

It might not be as obvious as you think it is. It's easy to assume he's aware of what you need—and he's choosing to ignore you—but it could be that he's simply oblivious. So give him the chance to meet your needs by spelling out, slowly and lovingly, what you'd like from him.

Differentiate
what you *need*
from
what you *want*.

These two can be easily confused. But there is a difference—a big difference, actually. Not that wants aren't important, but they should come second to needs and are best kept in the "optional" category.

Welcome him into **your world.**

Don't keep him at a distance. Encourage him to be part of what you're doing and how you think. Make your world a warm, welcoming place for him to be.

GIVE UP
your *need*
to be right.

It's not as bad as it sounds. Give it up and you'll be glad you did. Being right is a highly overrated position.

Pray through problems.

Don't work them out on your own. If we are believers in Christ, then we are not left to figure out our problems by ourselves, in our own strength. No, we have an all-powerful, all-knowing God to Whom we can turn. (See Romans 8:26.)

Convince him
that he's the
man of your dreams.

And he'll become that man.

Give thanks.

Always. For all things. (See Ephesians 5:20.)

Choosing to be thankful can truly transform your life and your marriage. Try it. Express your gratefulness to your husband —pick one wonderful quality and then another— and mention it to others around you too. Start telling him the things you appreciate about him and be sure you believe what you're saying. Watch how this one practice changes you and impacts him.

Make the
MOST
of little
moments.

Don't wait for those great sweeping events—those are mostly found in the movies. Big love stories are made up of many small, behind-the-scenes moments.

Gratefully accept his gifts.

Don't mention the price or how he got it "wrong." This isn't the time to be practical or point out that it's not the right size or color. Just be grateful.

ALWAYS
remain *lovers*.

Do the kinds of things that lovers do. Touch him as you pass in the hall. Reach for him in the middle of the night. Turn up the heat and turn down the music. Slow dance. Kiss and hang on tightly.

Judge him not.

"That you be not judged" (Matt. 7:1 NKJV). Besides, it's a much stronger position to stand by his side than to sit in judgment over him.

Hold hands.

Grab his hand when you're walking together or when you're driving together or when you're simply sitting side by side on the couch. Reach for his hand for no reason at all. It's such a simple way to express connection. Two people joined together hand in hand going through life together.

Here's a number for you: 10,579.

A somewhat surprising number, isn't it?

Rather amazing. That's how many times, I've calculated, that my husband and I have held hands. Over 10,000 times. My slim hand tucked into his large, strong one. Our fingers entwined and my wedding ring tucked in between. The fact that we've been married for over twenty-five years may help account for this impressive number.

But then again . . . maybe it doesn't explain a thing.

You should be shocked that we hold hands at all. You see, the odds were against us from the get-go.

"Those two will wake up hating each other."

That's what the pastor pronounced at our wedding ceremony. He really did. Now he didn't say it publicly—merely mentioned it casually afterward to those standing nearby. In his professional opinion, we didn't stand a chance.

Wake up hating? Not exactly the blessing a new bride looks for on her wedding day. It seemed we were doomed. Declared incompatible from the very start.

Then, oh, how I dreaded that day when we'd wake up hating each other. I'd always hoped we'd turn out the lights loving one another. And wake up just the same. Every day for the rest of our lives.

A few years went by and we looked on while many of our friends' marriages fell apart. He and I lay next to each other one night in the dark, quietly praying and weeping for them. Our hearts breaking for their hearts—and for their children's. Divorce wasn't what anyone ever wanted.

And I wept a little from fear too. *What would happen to us? Were we going to be next?*

As if he could read my thoughts, he grasped my hand and whispered, "Let's not do that, babe. Let's love each other instead." That's all he said. But I knew what he meant, and I squeezed his hand back to let him know he could count me in. We were going up against the odds.

Now here we are, so many years later and still holding hands. Still learning to love each other. Still determined never to grow cold or hateful toward each other. Yes, by God's grace, I'm still reaching for his hand.

Celebrate your anniversary.

Do something special together and recognize the grand occasion that it is. You don't have to do anything fancy or expensive, just make it thoughtful and memorable. Do the same thing each year. Or maybe your tradition can be to do something different each year.

Don't hang out with friends who put him— or their own husbands— down.

Such behavior is so destructive. Let your friends know you love them, but you are incredibly loyal when it comes to your man. You won't stand for put-downs or critical remarks. If they love you, they'll want to support you and your marriage.

Tell him
how *attracted*
you are to him.

Let him know about the magnetic pull you feel toward him. He wants to hear you're drawn to him as much as you want to hear he's drawn to you.

Back him up
in his
decision-making.

He'll value your support. As much as possible, go with his lead. This will give him confidence and, most likely, make it that much easier—if or when—you do disagree with him. He'll be more likely to listen to and respect you because he knows you wouldn't go against it without good reason.

The *Lord* can heal your hurts.

Your husband cannot. So don't resent him for something he can't do. (See Psalm 147:3.)

Write
little
love notes.

Tuck them in his lunch. Or write on the bathroom mirror. Send a text or a quick email. Passing secret love notes never goes out of style.

Embrace your differences.

If you were both the same, how boring would that be? So rather than trying to form him into a male version of yourself, be glad you each have your own unique strengths and personality.

Express *enthusiasm* for his plans and ideas.

Worry about the practical application and serious possibilities later. Let your first response be positive and encouraging! That's what gives him courage to try new things and consider new adventures.

Keep tenderness
in your *love.*

Don't let hardness or sharpness creep in to make it brittle.
Protect your love from outside pressures and stresses that
can spill over into your relationship with him.

ALWAYS
choose love—
again and again.

Love suffers long and is kind; love does not envy; love does not parade itself, is not puffed up; does not behave rudely, does not seek its own, is not provoked, thinks no evil; does not rejoice in iniquity, but rejoices in the truth; bears all things, believes all things, hopes all things, endures all things.

Love never fails. (1 Cor. 13:4–8 NKJV)

Hard to believe.

Here it's been over twenty-five years since that handsome, blue-eyed, boot-wearing man walked into the room. Into my life. He still wears his Levi's and those thick, manly sweaters. We still manage to get lost in conversation. And he still occasionally plays that old Billy Joel song for me—just to see if I remember.

And I do.

And always will.

Yet some things have changed. I'd like to think we've come a long way since we first met at that dinner party. I've learned so much about this man I married, about being his wife, and about enjoying a great marriage together. A lasting love.

Like you, we're on a lifelong journey of learning to love each other.

Lisa Jacobson studied abroad in Paris and Israel and lived in mud huts in Cameroon before marrying Matt and raising and home-educating their eight children in the Pacific Northwest. She is a graduate of Willamette University and has an MA from Western Seminary. In 2012, Lisa began Club31Women.com, a writing, mentoring, and speaking ministry that has grown into a powerful voice for biblical womanhood. She is also the author of *100 Words of Affirmation Your Husband Needs to Hear.*

Matt and Lisa host the popular *FAITHFUL LIFE* podcast, focusing on what it means to be a biblical Christian in marriage, parenting, church, and culture.

Simple, Loving Words to Encourage Your Child
EVERY DAY

Matt and Lisa Jacobson want you to discover the powerful ways you can build up your child in love. These books offer you one hundred things to say that will help your son or daughter feel empowered, inspired, and deeply loved.

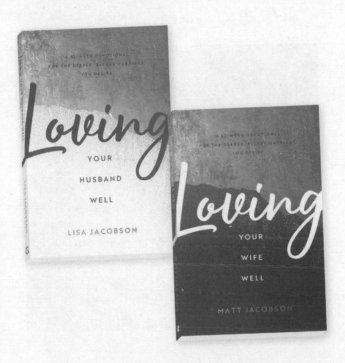

Connect with
Lisa and Club31Women!

Club31Women.com

Cohost of the *FAITHFUL LIFE* Podcast

@Club31Women